2 Writing Words

Writing *a*, *b*, *c*, and *d* Words

■ Read the word aloud. Then say the sound of each letter as you trace it.

Name

W9-BOL-845

Date

To parents

On the following pages, your child will learn to link lowercase letters. Before your child begins writing, please ask him or her to read the words. If your child seems has difficulty, try saying the word together as he or she traces it. When your child completes each exercise, praise him or her.

ant

ant   *ant*   *ant*

bat

bat   *bat*   *bat*

cub

cub   *cub*   *cub*

dog

dog   *dog*   *dog*

Writing *a*, *b*, *c*, and *d* Words

■ Read the word aloud.
  Then say the sound of each letter as you trace and write it.

ant

ant

ant   *ant*

bat

bat

bat   *bat*

cub

cub

cub   *cub*

dog

dog

dog   *dog*

Review
Writing *a - z*

Name	
Date	

■ Trace the letters a to z. Say the sound of the letter as you trace it.

To parents
Do not be concerned if your child cannot write the letters perfectly at first. He or she will gradually be able to do so after repeated practice. When your child is finished, offer praise, such as, "Nice work!"

a   b   c   d

e   f   g   h

i   j   k   l

m   n   o   p

q   r   s   t

u   v   w   x

y   z

Writing a - z

■ Trace the letters A to Z. Say the sound of the letter as you trace it.

A  B  C  D

E  F  G  H

I  J  K  L

M  N  O  P

Q R S T

U V W X

Y Z

Writing Words

Writing *e*, *f*, *g*, and *h* Words

Name

Date

■ Read the word aloud. Then say the sound of each letter as you trace it.

To parents
If your child has difficulty writing the words when there are no lines to trace, do not be concerned. It is okay if your child does not write each word perfectly. When your child is finished, offer lots of praise.

egg

egg *egg* *egg*

fox

fox *fox* *fox*

get

get *get* *get*

hat

hat *hat* *hat*

Writing *e*, *f*, *g*, and *h* Words

▪ Read the word aloud.
  Then say the sound of each letter as you trace and write it.

egg

egg

egg

fox

fox

fox

get

get

get

hat

hat

hat

Writing Words

Writing *i, j, k,* and *l* Words

■Read the word aloud. Then say the sound of each letter as you trace it.

ink

ink   *ink*   *ink*

jog

jog   *jog*   *jog*

kid

kid   *kid*   *kid*

leg

leg   *leg*   *leg*

Writing *i*, *j*, *k*, and *l* Words

■ Read the word aloud.
  Then say the sound of each letter as you trace and write it.

ink

ink

ink   *ink*

jog

jog

jog   *jog*

kid

kid

kid   *kid*

leg

leg

leg   *leg*

Review

Writing *a* - *l* Words

Name

Date

■ Read the word aloud. Then say the sound of each letter as you trace it.

ant

egg

ink

bat

fox

jog

cub

get

kid

dog

hat

leg

Writing *a - l* Words

■Read the word aloud. Then say the sound of each letter as you write it.

ant

egg

ink

bat

fox

jog

cub

get

kid

dog

hat

leg

6 Writing Words

Writing *m, n, o,* and *p* Words

Name

Date

■ Read the word aloud. Then say the sound of each letter as you trace it.

mix

nap

one

pig

Writing *m, n, o,* and *p* Words

■ Read the word aloud.
  Then say the sound of each letter as you trace and write it.

mix

mix

mix   *mix*

nap

nap

nap   *nap*

one

one

one   *one*

pig

pig

pig   *pig*

7 Writing Words

Writing q, r, s, and t Words

■Read the word aloud. Then say the sound of each letter as you trace it.

quiz

 quiz quiz

red

 red red

six

 six six

tub

 tub tub

Writing q, r, s, and t Words

■ Read the word aloud.
  Then say the sound of each letter as you trace and write it.

quiz

quiz

quiz   *quiz*

red

red

red   *red*

six

six

six   *six*

tub

tub

tub   *tub*

Writing Words

Writing u, v, w, and x Words

Name

Date

■ Read the word aloud. Then say the sound of each letter as you trace it.

up

van

wet

box

Writing *u, v, w,* and *x* Words

■ Read the word aloud.
  Then say the sound of each letter as you trace and write it.

up

up

up   *up*

van

van

van   *van*

wet

wet

wet   *wet*

box

box

box   *box*

Review

Writing m - x Words

■Read the word aloud. Then say the sound of each letter as you trace it.

mix

quiz

up

nap

red

van

one

six

wet

pig

tub

box

Writing *m* - *x* Words

■ Read the word aloud. Then say the sound of each letter as you write it.

mix

quiz

up

nap

red

van

1· *one*

6⋮⋮ *six*

wet

pig

tub

box

10 **Writing Words**

Writing y and z Words

Name

Date

■ Read the word aloud.
  Then say the sound of each letter as you trace and write it.

yak

yak

zoo

zoo

Writing *y* and *z* Words

■ Read the word aloud.
  Then say the sound of each letter as you trace and write it.

yak

zoo

yak

zoo

Writing Words

Writing *a*, *b*, *c*, and *d* Words

■ Read the word aloud. Then say the sound of each letter as you trace it.

To parents
On the following pages, your child will link lowercase letters to create longer words. Before your child begins writing, please ask him or her to read the words on the page. If your child has difficulty, try saying the word together as he or she traces it. When your child completes each exercise, praise him or her.

aunt

aunt   aunt   aunt

bone

bone   bone   bone

clay

clay   clay   clay

dune

dune   dune   dune

Writing *a*, *b*, *c*, and *d* Words

■ Read the word aloud.
  Then say the sound of each letter as you trace and write it.

aunt

aunt

aunt   *aunt*

bone

bone

bone   *bone*

clay

clay

clay   *clay*

dune

dune

dune   *dune*

Name
Date

■Read the word aloud. Then say the sound of each letter as you trace it.

eight **8** ∷ ∷

frog

girl

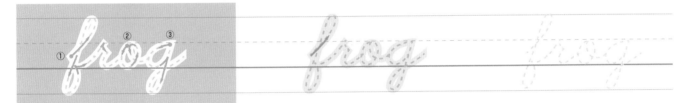

hide

Writing *e*, *f*, *g*, and *h* Words

■ Read the word aloud.
  Then say the sound of each letter as you trace and write it.

eight **8** ⋮⋮⋮⋮⋮   *eight*

eight   *eight*

frog   *frog*

frog   *frog*

girl   *girl*

girl   *girl*

hide   *hide*

hide   *hide*

Writing Words

Writing *i*, *j*, *k*, and *l* Words

Name
Date

■ Read the word aloud. Then say the sound of each letter as you trace it.

itch

jump

kite

lion

Writing *i, j, k,* and *l* Words

■ Read the word aloud.
   Then say the sound of each letter as you trace and write it.

itch

itch

itch

jump

jump

jump

kite

kite

kite

lion

lion

lion

Review

Writing *a* - *ℓ* Words

Name
Date

■ Read the word aloud. Then say the sound of each letter as you trace it.

aunt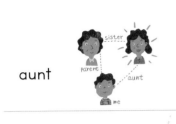

eight

itch

bone

frog

jump

clay

girl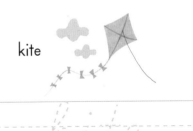

kite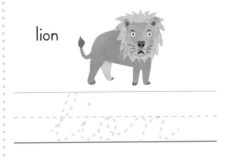

dune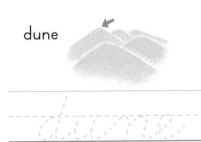

hide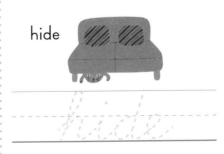

lion

Writing *a - l* Words

■Read the word aloud. Then say the sound of each letter as you write it.

aunt

eight

itch

bone

frog

jump

clay

girl

kite

dune

hide

lion

15 Writing Words

Writing *m, n, o,* and *p* Words

Name

Date

■ Read the word aloud. Then say the sound of each letter as you trace it.

meet

meet   *meet*   *meet*

newt

newt   *newt*   *newt*

open

open   *open*   *open*

play

play   *play*   *play*

Writing *m, n, o*, and *p* Words

■Read the word aloud.
  Then say the sound of each letter as you trace and write it.

meet

meet

meet

newt

newt

newt

open

open

open

play

play

play

16 Writing Words

Writing *q, r, s,* and *t* Words

■Read the word aloud. Then say the sound of each letter as you trace it.

queen

queen   queen   queen

rose

rose   rose   rose

sled

sled   sled   sled

tent

tent   tent   tent

Writing *q, r, s,* and *t* Words

■ Read the word aloud.
  Then say the sound of each letter as you trace and write it.

queen

queen

queen

rose

rose

rose

sled

sled

sled

tent

tent

tent

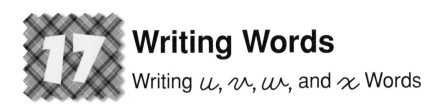

Writing Words

Writing u, v, w, and x Words

Name
Date

■ Read the word aloud. Then say the sound of each letter as you trace it.

uncle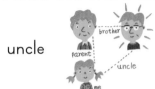

vest

wink

xylem

Writing *u*, *v*, *w*, and *x* Words

■ Read the word aloud.
  Then say the sound of each letter as you trace and write it.

uncle

uncle

uncle

vest

vest

vest

wink

wink

wink

xylem

xylem

xylem

Review

Writing *m* - *x* Words

■ Read the word aloud. Then say the sound of each letter as you trace it.

meet

queen

uncle

newt

rose

vest

open

sled

wink

play

tent

xylem

Writing *m - x* Words

■Read the word aloud. Then say the sound of each letter as you write it.

meet

queen

uncle

newt

rose

vest

open

sled

wink

play

tent

xylem

Name	
Date	

■ Read the word aloud.
Then say the sound of each letter as you trace and write it.

yell

yell

yell

yell

yell

zebra

zebra

zebra

zebra

zebra

Writing *y* and *z* Words

■Read the word aloud.
  Then say the sound of each letter as you trace and write it.

yell

zebra

yell

zebra

Writing Words

Writing *A*, *B*, and *C* Words

Name

Date

■ Read each sentence aloud. Then say the sound of each letter as you trace it.

To parents
From this page on, your child will learn to link uppercase and lowercase letters together. Before your child begins writing, please ask him or her to read the sentences. If your child has difficulty, try saying the words together while pointing at each word. Even if your child cannot read or write the words perfectly at first, he or she will gradually be able to do so after repeated practice.

Ants like apples.

Ants like apples.

Ants like apples.

Bees make honey.

Bees make honey.

Bees make honey.

Caves are dark.

Caves are dark.

Caves are dark.

Writing a, B, and C Words

■ Read each sentence aloud.
  Then say the sound of each letter as you trace and write it.

Ants like apples.

Ants like apples.

Ants

like apples.

Bees make honey.

Bees make honey.

Bees

make honey.

Caves are dark.

Caves are dark.

Caves

are dark.

21 Writing Words

Writing _D_, _E_, and _F_ Words

Name

Date

■ Read each sentence aloud. Then say the sound of each letter as you trace it.

To parents
Now your child is writing words in a sentence. If your child has difficulty reading the sentence, try asking him or her to describe the picture. Then read the sentence aloud together while pointing at each word.

Dogs chew on bones.

Dogs chew on bones.

Dogs chew on bones.

Elks eat grass.

Elks eat grass.

Elks eat grass.

Fish have fins.

Fish have fins.

Fish have fins.

Writing D, E, and F Words

■ Read each sentence aloud.
  Then say the sound of each letter as you trace and write it.

Dogs chew on bones.

Dogs chew on bones.

Dogs

chew on bones.

Elks eat grass.

Elks eat grass.

Elks

eat grass.

Fish have fins.

Fish have fins.

Fish

have fins.

22 Writing Words

Writing *G*, *H*, and *I* Words

Name

Date

■ Read each sentence aloud. Then say the sound of each letter as you trace it.

Gum is sticky.

Gum is sticky.

Gum is sticky.

Hats cover your head.

Hats cover your head.

Hats cover your head.

Ice cream is a treat.

Ice cream is a treat.

Ice cream is a treat.

Writing *G, H,* and *I* Words

■ Read each sentence aloud.
Then say the sound of each letter as you trace and write it.

Gum is sticky.

Gum is sticky.

Gum

is sticky.

Hats cover your head.

Hats cover your head.

Hats

cover your head.

Ice cream is a treat.

Ice cream is a treat.

Ice

cream is a treat.

23 Review

Writing 𝒶 - 𝓁 Words

Name

Date

■ Read each sentence aloud. Then say the sound of each letter as you trace it.

Ants like apples.

Bees make honey.

Caves are dark.

Dogs chew on bones.

Elk eat grass.

Fish have fins.

Gum is sticky.

Hats cover your head.

Ice cream is a treat.

Writing 𝒶 - 𝓁 Words

■Read each sentence aloud. Then say the sound of each letter as you write it.

Ants
like apples.

Bees
make honey.

Caves
are dark.

Dogs
chew on bones.

Elks
eat grass.

Fish
have fins.

Gum
is sticky.

Hats
cover your head.

Ice
cream is a treat.

Writing Words

Writing *J*, *K*, and *L* Words

Name
Date

■ Read each sentence aloud. Then say the sound of each letter as you trace it.

Jam is spread on bread.

Jam is spread on bread.

Jam is spread on bread.

Kites soar in the air.

Kites soar in the air.

Kites soar in the air.

Lions can roar.

Lions can roar.

Lions can roar.

Writing $\mathcal{J}$, $\mathcal{K}$, and $\mathcal{L}$ Words

- Read each sentence aloud.
  Then say the sound of each letter as you trace and write it.

Jam is spread on bread.

Jam is spread on bread.

Jam

is spread on bread.

Kites soar in the air.

Kites soar in the air.

Kites

soar in the air.

Lions can roar.

Lions can roar.

Lions

can roar.

Writing Words

Writing M, N, and O Words

Name

Date

■ Read each sentence aloud. Then say the sound of each letter as you trace it.

Mice like cheese.

Mice like cheese.

Mice like cheese.

Nuts are a healthy snack.

Nuts are a healthy snack.

Nuts are a healthy snack.

Owls stay awake at night.

Owls stay awake at night.

Owls stay awake at night.

Writing $\mathcal{M}$, $\mathcal{N}$, and $\mathcal{O}$ Words

■ Read each sentence aloud.
Then say the sound of each letter as you trace and write it.

Mice like cheese.

Mice like cheese.

Mice

like cheese.

Nuts are a healthy snack.

Nuts are a healthy snack.

Nuts

are a healthy snack.

Owls stay awake at night.

Owls stay awake at night.

Owls

stay awake at night.

26 Writing Words

Writing *P*, *Q*, and *R* Words

Name

Date

To parents
If your child encounters difficulty writing the words, encourage your child to write slowly and follow the tracing lines. Offer your child lots of praise when he or she finishes each exercise.

■ Read each sentence aloud. Then say the sound of each letter as you trace it.

Pianos have keys.

Pianos have keys.

Pianos have keys.

Quilts are warm.

Quilts are warm.

Quilts are warm.

Rain falls from the sky.

Rain falls from the sky.

Rain falls from the sky.

Writing *P*, *2*, and *R* Words

■ Read each sentence aloud.
   Then say the sound of each letter as you trace and write it.

Pianos have keys.

Pianos have keys.

Pianos

have keys.

Quilts are warm.

Quilts are warm.

Quilts

are warm.

Rain falls from the sky.

Rain falls from the sky.

Rain

falls from the sky.

Review

Writing J - R Words

■Read each sentence aloud. Then say the sound of each letter as you trace it.

Jam is spread on bread.

Kites soar in the air.

Lions can roar.

Mice like cheese.

Nuts are a healthy snack.

Owls stay awake at night.

Pianos have keys.

Quilts are warm.

Rain falls from the sky.

■Read each sentence aloud. Then say the sound of each letter as you write it.

Jam
is spread on bread.

Kites
soar in the air.

Lions
can roar.

Mice
like cheese.

Nuts
are a healthy snack.

Owls
stay awake at night.

Pianos
have keys.

Quilts
are warm.

Rain
falls from the sky.

Writing Words

Writing *S*, *T*, and *U* Words

Date

■ Read each sentence aloud. Then say the sound of each letter as you trace it.

Soap cleans your skin.

Soap cleans your skin.

Soap cleans your skin.

Tacos are tasty.

Tacos are tasty.

Tacos are tasty.

Utah is in the United States.

Utah is in the United States.

Utah is in the United States.

Writing *S*, *T*, and *U* Words

55

Writing *S*, *T*, and *U* Words

■ Read each sentence aloud.
   Then say the sound of each letter as you trace and write it.

Soap cleans your skin.

Soap cleans your skin.

Soap

cleans your skin.

Tacos are tasty.

Tacos are tasty.

Tacos

are tasty.

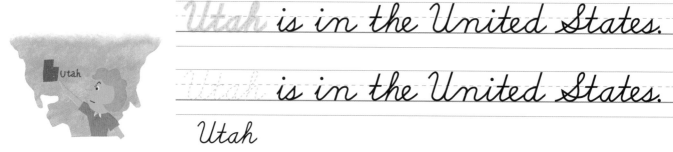

Utah is in the United States.

Utah is in the United States.

Utah

is in the United States.

Writing Words

Writing V, W, and X Words

Name

Date

■ Read each sentence aloud. Then say the sound of each letter as you trace it.

Vines can grow up walls.

Vines can grow up walls.

Vines can grow up walls.

Wind can carry seeds.

Wind can carry seeds.

Wind can carry seeds.

X-rays show your bones.

X-rays show your bones.

X-rays show your bones.

Writing V, W, and X Words

■ Read each sentence aloud.
Then say the sound of each letter as you trace and write it.

Vines can grow up walls.

Vines can grow up walls.

Vines

can grow up walls.

Wind can carry seeds.

Wind can carry seeds.

Wind

can carry seeds.

X-rays show your bones.

X-rays show your bones.

X-rays

show your bones.

Writing Words

Writing *Y* and *Z* Words

Name

Date

■ Read each sentence aloud. Then say the sound of each letter as you trace it.

Yaks have long hair.

Yaks have long hair.

Yaks have long hair.

Zoos have many animals.

Zoos have many animals.

Zoos have many animals.

Writing *Y* and *Z* Words

■ Read each sentence aloud.
  Then say the sound of each letter as you trace and write it.

Yaks have long hair.

Yaks have long hair.

Yaks

have long hair.

Zoos have many animals.

Zoos have many animals.

Zoos

have many animals.

Review

Writing *S* - *Z* Words

Name	
Date	

■ Read each sentence aloud. Then say the sound of each letter as you trace it.

Soap cleans your skin.

Tacos are tasty.

Utah is in the United States.

Vines can grow up walls.

Wind can carry seeds.

X-rays show your bones.

Yaks have long hair.

Zoos have many animals.

Writing *S - Z* Words

■Read each sentence aloud. Then say the sound of each letter as you write it.

Soap
    cleans your skin.

Tacos
    are tasty.

Utah
    is in the United States.

Vines
    can grow up walls.

Wind
    can carry seeds.

X-rays
    show your bones.

Yaks
    have long hair.

Zoos
    have many animals.

Review

Writing *a – m* Words

Name	
Date	

■ Read the word aloud. Then say the sound of each letter as you trace it.

ant

fox

kid

bat

get

leg

cub

hat

mix

dog

ink

egg

jog

Writing *a - m* Words

■ Read the word aloud. Then say the sound of each letter as you write it.

ant

fox

kid

bat

get

leg

cub

hat

mix

dog

ink

egg

jog

Review

Writing *n - z* Words

■ Read the word aloud. Then say the sound of each letter as you trace it.

nap

six

box

one

tub

yak

pig

up

zoo

quiz

van

red

wet

Writing *n - z* Words

■Read the word aloud. Then say the sound of each letter as you write it.

nap

six

box

one

tub

yak

pig

up

zoo

quiz

van

red

wet

Name
Date

■Read the word aloud. Then say the sound of each letter as you trace it.

aunt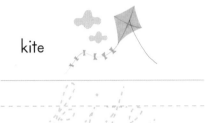

frog

kite

bone

girl

lion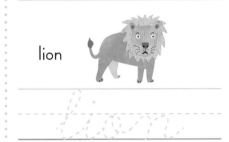

clay

hide

meet

dune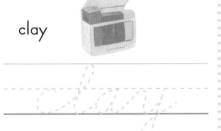

itch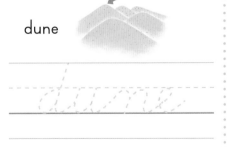

eight **8 ::::**

jump

Writing *a - m* Words

■Read the word aloud. Then say the sound of each letter as you write it.

aunt

frog

kite

bone

girl

lion

clay

hide

meet

dune

itch

eight

jump

35 Review

Writing *n - z* Words

Name
Date

■ Read the word aloud. Then say the sound of each letter as you trace it.

newt

sled

xylem

open

tent

yell

play

uncle

brother
parent
me uncle

zebra

queen

vest

rose

wink

Writing *n - z* Words

■Read the word aloud. Then say the sound of each letter as you write it.

newt

sled

xylem

open

tent

yell

play

uncle

zebra

queen

vest

rose

wink

36 Review

Writing a - l Words

Name

Date

■ Read each sentence aloud. Then say the sound of each letter as you trace it.

Ants like apples.

Bees make honey.

Caves are dark.

Dogs chew on bones.

Elk eat grass.

Fish have fins.

Gum is sticky.

Hats cover your head.

Ice cream is a treat.

Writing a - I Words

■Read each sentence aloud. Then say the sound of each letter as you write it.

Ants
like apples.

Bees
make honey.

Caves
are dark.

Dogs
chew on bones.

Elks
eat grass.

Fish
have fins.

Gum
is sticky.

Hats
cover your head.

Ice
cream is a treat.

Review

Writing *J - R* Words

■ Read each sentence aloud. Then say the sound of each letter as you trace it.

Jam is spread on bread.

Kites soar in the air.

Lions can roar.

Mice like cheese.

Nuts are a healthy snack.

Owls stay awake at night.

Pianos have keys.

Quilts are warm.

Rain falls from the sky.

Writing J - R Words

■ Read each sentence aloud. Then say the sound of each letter as you write it.

Jam

is spread on bread.

Kites

soar in the air.

Lions

can roar.

Mice

like cheese.

Nuts

are a healthy snack.

Owls

stay awake at night.

Pianos

have keys.

Quilts

are warm.

Rain

falls from the sky.

Review

Writing *S - Z* Words

■ Read each sentence aloud. Then say the sound of each letter as you trace it.

Soap cleans your skin.

Tacos are tasty.

Utah is in the United States.

Vines can grow up walls.

Wind can carry seeds.

X-rays show your bones.

Yaks have long hair.

Zoos have many animals.

Writing *S - Z* Words

■ Read each sentence aloud. Then say the sound of each letter as you write it.

Soap
cleans your skin.

Tacos
are tasty.

Utah
is in the United States.

Vines
can grow up walls.

Wind
can carry seeds.

X-rays
show your bones.

Yaks
have long hair.

Zoos
have many animals.

39 Review

Writing *a – m* Words

■ Read the word aloud. Then say the sound of each letter as you write it.

aunt

fox

kid

bone

girl

leg

cub

hat

mix

dune

ink

egg

jump

Writing *n - z* Words

■ Read the word aloud. Then say the sound of each letter as you write it.

newt

sled

xylem

one

tub

yak

pig

uncle

zebra

quiz

vest

rose

wet

KUM⊙N

Certificate of Achievement

_____

is hereby congratulated on completing

My Book of CURSIVE WRITING: WORDS

Presented on _____ , 20 _____

_____
Parent or Guardian